SNIPPETS OF *Truths*

Memories of a Southern Childhood

BY

MARY HARDY

iUniverse, Inc.
Bloomington

Snippets of Truths
Memories of a Southern Childhood

iUniverse books may be ordered through booksellers or by contacting:

iUniverse
1663 Liberty Drive
Bloomington, IN 47403
www.iuniverse.com
1-800-Authors (1-800-288-4677)

ISBN: 978-1-4759-8449-1 (sc)
ISBN: 978-1-4759-8450-7 (ebk)

Printed in the United States of America

iUniverse rev. date: 04/25/2013

SNIPPETS OF *Truths*

Dedication

This book is dedicated to my spouse, parents, siblings, children, and grandchildren.

CONTENTS

ACKNOWLEDGMENTS

I want to thank my husband and friend, Charles Hardy, for encouraging me to work and write when I did not feel like writing. He always knew to say the right words to inspire me to write just one more snippet of truth.

INTRODUCTION

The snippets of truths contained in this book are based on true events as I remember them. They relate to and reflect my childhood experiences growing up in South Mississippi. While they are my experiences, the folks remaining in the small community still reminisce about and discuss them often.

The anecdotes included in this book are *my* snippets, but they could very well remind you, the reader, of times worth sharing in your life. The snippets could be triggers for your own storytelling, no matter how young or old you are. As you read the book, take notes in the spaces provided and make plans to share your own story. Several of the names included in the text have been changed to protect the innocent.

The snippets are not shared in a chronological order, but the way memory revisits the past, at random.

1

Girl, You Have Pretty Legs

For as long as I can remember, Auntee told me I had pretty legs. The message has stuck with me, and in my memory, it is still as strong as cement. I remember it as vividly as if Auntee had told me yesterday. When I put on stockings, which I barely wear, I whisper to myself, "You have pretty legs." Those words of approval give me the courage to show my legs with grace and confidence. I wear dresses of any length, slacks, or shorts without being self-conscious. This confidence is floating within me like air. It is always there.

Notes:

2

Standing Upright in the Cotton Field

The ladies mentioned in this snippet are members of a small community in a southern town who worked together in the field during the farming season. There was always plenty of chatter, singing, storytelling, and laughter among the group. They had control of many acts of persistence, but one was a perfect art.

Standing upright in the cotton field was an art, and the ladies at work in the field had it mastered. They did not hide when they had to go. They stood, pulled their dress to the front and slightly to the back, and let the water flow. It was an amazing act, soft and quick—as quick as the blink of an eye. Those of us working with them in the field wanted to do it too, but we were not as skilled as they were. They had practiced it so many times it seemed to come naturally. There were no toilets in the field, so you either had to acquire that talent, toot to the person behind you or go to the bushes. Standing upright in the cotton field was the great art of practiced necessity.

Notes:

3

Take Your Sardine Can Home

When we worked away from home and had to buy our dinner from a store nearby, we would often buy sardines and crackers. The combination was a filling meal that would keep us from getting hungry throughout the evening. My aunt would tell us that if she ate them, she had to take the sardine can home with her. Sardines carry a fishy aroma that you can't erase quickly without a bath. Therefore, without a bath, she would smell like fish and would definitely have to explain it to her spouse. I didn't quite understand, and the story has stayed with me over the years.

Notes:

4

Ole Bossy Gal

Ole Bossy Gal was a stately animal. I am not sure why she was given her name, but she was definitely the boss. As the boss, herding the cattle and keeping up with the children of the family was a great part of her job. She was tall and slender with shaggy dark brown hair. Her place was inside the house as a housedog or outside as a survivor. She could adapt to either place.

She was like a member of the family, a true family dog. Her masters were my aunt and uncle and their six children. She followed them everywhere, guarding them, even if they worked in the garden or in the fields at the edge of the farm. Ole Bossy Gal was the boss; she would make every step her family made, wagging her tail all along, and would bark if protection was needed. She lived to be very old—in dog years, anyway. We were very sad when she died. It seemed as if we had lost a best friend. And we had.

Notes:

5

Sweater in the Summertime

Auntee wore a sweater in the summer months of June and July. As I remember, the sweater was white wool with a worn, creamy texture. It would fall near her waist and meet at the front where a button would hold it tight. I can still see her walking in the front yard near the pecan trees lined sparingly near the front of the house, facing the gravel road. Summer after summer I would watch a mystery: a lady about to faint. During my adult years it has become clear to me what was happening to her. As you get older, your body temperature changes, and you are cold when it is hot. I did not understand what was happening, but I think I do now. Do you?

Notes:

6

Auntee

Auntee was a brave, honest, and courageous lady who always had a song to sing and a poem to say. She was never at a loss for words. She could rise to any occasion. I always wanted to be like her when it came to captivating an audience.

She was brave when it came to style of dress. She knew what she wanted to wear and how she wanted it to fit. If she had a dress and it was not designed in the style she wanted, she would alter it. She would do the same for her hat by adding a bow or turning the brim up or down. Auntee was brave enough to wear a ponytail when ponytails were not fashionable for mature ladies. She told us that once, when she was wearing a ponytail, an older lady told her that she was too old to wear her hair in that style. She did it anyway. I wish she were alive today to see that I—and many others—wear a ponytail almost every day.

Auntee was always honest. She would openly tell you what she was thinking, and we took her thoughts like big girls. I always stopped by to visit with her and Uncle Hubbard when I visited my parents. On this particular day, soon after my youngest daughter was born, I stopped by to show her my new baby. When I pulled the blanket back so she could take a peek, she immediately told me that she was ugly. I took it like a champ. As my daughter grew up to become a young lady, Auntee would often tell me that she turned out to be a beautiful girl.

Notes:

7

Tenth-Grade Class

I remember the day when the world was told that President John F. Kennedy had been assassinated as if it was yesterday. Everything and everyone came to a sudden and silent halt. It was as if the world had ended. I was sitting at my desk in a Mississippi history class with twenty-five other students. Our teacher was standing at the chalkboard, sharing the information with the class. If we were talking at all, we stopped. After a while, we continued our class discussion, but with focus on the president.

Notes:

8

Majorette

Dancing has never been easy for me. I am not coordinated enough to make the different motions and moves look smooth. As everyone knows, to become a majorette, you have to learn to dance for an audience. I learned to move enough to get on the football field at halftime for the show. While it is amazing, it also shows that you can do everything you want or need to do if you do not have a choice. I did not have a choice because it was the only way for me to attend a football game. My father was not going to take me to an after-school activity unless I was a participant. So I participated—as a dancer.

Notes:

9

Homecoming Queen

The fitted red wool dress fit my slim body perfectly, and the furry black tam hat looked good on me. My mama designed and sewed the red wool dress, while I bought the fur hat at Stephen's local department store. I don't remember the type and style of shoes I wore anymore, but I am sure they came from the same store and were appropriate for the occasion. I was the cutest person on the court. This was in my senior year, and another opportunity to participate in a school function, so my daddy would drive me to school after regular hours.

Notes:

10

First Year of School

School has always been a joy for me, even in my first year. My mother had schooled me well. I could read and write even before I attended school, and my teacher thought this was exceptional. She attended church with us and knew my mother was teaching me, but she did not know that I was an accomplished student. It was a pleasant surprise. I did not like missing school and became very upset if the school bus came and I could not board it, which only happened if I was ill.

I had the same teacher for first grade and fourth grade. By fourth grade, I was even more accomplished. She had a typewriter in her classroom and insisted that I learn to type. When I made a mistake, she tapped my hands with strict insistence that I learn. To this day, typing is not one of my favorite activities.

Notes:

11

Third Grade and Raw Eggs

School was always an adventure for me, but third grade was a different experience altogether. I had a teacher who enjoyed eating raw eggs for lunch, and she did so openly and with sheer enjoyment. This teacher thought that I was very accomplished and wanted to send me on to fifth grade, but my mother would not settle for that suggestion. She thought that I was too small in stature to skip a grade, and so I moved to fourth grade with my classmates. It was a nice surprise to have my first-grade teacher again in fourth grade.

Notes:

12

Sixth Grade and the Grammar Jar

We had a well-spoken and caring sixth-grade teacher, and so sixth grade was a year of language refinement. Our teacher insisted that this was our last chance to achieve our goal of speaking and writing well, a goal she felt had to be accomplished. One of her teaching tools was a glass quart jar on her medium-size wooden desk. If you chopped or misused a word, you had to place a penny in the jar. I don't remember what we bought with the money, but we might have replaced her desk and chair. I often think of my sixth-grade teacher with gratitude for being persistent and supportive of her students.

Notes:

13

Math and Life

My math teacher shared many life lessons during the school year. He had a story to fit every occasion and the same great attitude. He would smile even when he was not having a good day. He was a great teacher of math and just as great if not better when he was teaching a life lesson. Math was not my strength, but I could not wait to get to his class to hear what he had to tell us. I sat near a close friend who was a math expert, and she helped to make math real for me.

Christmas was an event for the math teacher. He would purchase enough oranges for his math students. He was an awesome thinker and a generous person. He cared for his students and wanted them to become lifelong learners and wholesome, well-rounded individuals.

Notes:

14

High School English Teacher

High school English was a requirement to graduate from high school. Then, as now, you cannot choose your teachers. Our English teacher, the wife of a preacher, was unique. She was well versed in the language and proud of the fact that she had it mastered. She spoke with style and grace. I can still see her today as she sauntered gracefully into the classroom, dressed in a two-piece suit with high-heeled shoes, stockings, and well-groomed, perfectly dyed hair without even a touch of gray. Her favorite lesson was diagramming sentences; I never quite saw a purpose for this assignment, but I hope that I absorbed her lessons. Somehow, I think I have taught myself what I know about the language by applying what I learned in my high school English class.

Notes:

15

Making Homemade Ice Cream

Summer was a time to enjoy being with friends and family—and to make ice cream. The ice cream was special because we made it with my mama's creative recipe. The ingredients—milk, eggs, sugar, and vanilla flavor—were blended with care and placed in a silver gallon molasses can with a top lid and handle. Then we placed the can in a bucket of ice salt and turned it continuously using the handle of the can. The process continued until the mixture was frozen, which would take several hours. We would serve the ice cream with homemade teacakes and enjoy it with friends and family on the long porch between the main bedrooms and the kitchen. There was always a breeze in this area, which was a pleasant atmosphere for eating the ice cream and teacakes. My mama didn't have to be concerned about the cleanup. We would pull out the straw broom, sweep the porch, and away we would go back to our chores or out to play.

Notes:

16

❖

Worried about My Sister

A day that started as usual, something unforeseen happened. Someone noticed a piece of fabric stuck in the outdoor restroom commode and reported it to the school administrators. They called in the fire department to pump the commode. We thought that a person might have fallen in, and those of us with sisters were worried because the incident had occurred in the girls' restroom. I was afraid that it was my sister and she was afraid that it was me because we could not find each other. In the end, after the commode was pumped clean, we learned that not a person but a piece of fabric had been stuck. However, it was great to know that the administrators cared so much and cleared up the situation quickly.

Notes:

17

Coca-Cola Bottle Dolls

There was always time to be creative and to play no matter what time of year it was. Using a small Coca-Cola bottle or another slender glass soda bottle, we would design the perfect doll with stylish hair as long or as short as we desired. The hair was made of brown fine twine and held in place inside the bottle with an appropriately sized corncob. When it was securely in place, we shaped, cut, curled, and styled the hair to our satisfaction. Sometimes we would get extra creative and make a skirt or a blouse for the doll from the twine or from oak-tree leaves. We played with the dolls until they were broken beyond repair.

Notes:

18

❖

Thoughts of Remembrance

Cannot remember you husband's name? Where you parked the car? What you wanted to get when you walked into the kitchen? Relax! Scientists say such memory lapses are natural, especially as you get older. Adults remember little, if anything, that happened to them before the age of five. When we reach our thirties, we typically begin to experience a drop in memory. I am neither five nor thirty, and my memory is somewhat intact. With the help of someone close to me, we put together a few remember-when anecdotes for my mom and dad for their fiftieth wedding anniversary.

Remember that prank on our parents of a friendly abduction of Louise, when she was taken to Uncle Hubbard's house in a burlap sack? How surprised Uncle Hubbard's family was when she stepped out of the sack and said, "Hi!" Remember when Carol followed Aunt Caroline home? That was a long walk. How did she go unnoticed? Remember when Pauline accidentally squeezed the baby chicks so tight that she destroyed them? She thought she was pampering them. Remember when Tom fed sand to the cats? They were afraid to come near the house. Remember when we were working in the field and Tom and Jerry were told to stop counting the birds—daydreaming—and keep up with the crew? We knew how to work smart by getting the work done at a pace where we would not get very tired. Remember when Janie, the renowned seamstress, learned how to sew like Mama? We all wanted her to make us a dress. I finally learned to sew when Mama would not sew for me. And remember when Earl drew football plays everywhere? He was only preparing for what he enjoys most—coaching football. He has made a productive career with that special ball. Remember when James would spend hours on the piano trying to learn a tune, preparing for his next in-house concert featuring the rare talent of his younger sister? He would occasionally invite a couple of friends or relatives to jam with him. We will never forget that original tune call "Shake It," cowritten and produced by Josh and James but never recorded. Mama and Daddy, how was the noise? Lastly, remember when the baby began to collect the beautiful semiformal and formal dresses? That was how the many beauty pageants our family hosted began. Those were the good ole days—and the beginning of another story.

Notes:

19

❈

Picking Peas and Cucumbers during the Summer

Peas and cucumbers were the fast cash crops in June and July. They grew fast and plentiful, which kept us busy. And the latter was exactly what Daddy wanted. We picked cucumbers for the market on Mondays, Wednesdays, and Fridays. Daddy would take them to what we called the cucumber vet for processing in the small town of Mt. Olive, Mississippi. We would often travel with him. In town, he would buy ice cream and sodas for us, and we would combine the two to make an ice cream soda float. If we did not ride with him, he would purchase the items and bring them with him so that we could make the floats at home. This was always such a treat. Mama also pickled and canned cucumbers in a jar for us to eat later during the winter months.

Pea picking was a delight. We picked them every day, some to sell and some for our own dinners and suppers. Shelling peas made your fingers turn purple and irritated them so much that they became tender. The pea-shelling activity didn't last long because we knew there was a new day to come and the process would start over again.

These chores helped us bond as a family because we worked together to get the job done. Selling peas and cucumbers helped my daddy and mama to have enough cash to purchase necessary items we did not produce on the farm.

Notes:

20

Dressed for the Sun

Growing up, we had to work the fields of our farm. Daddy always planted at least nine acres of cotton. He never said so, but we always figured that he planted one acre for each sibling to take care of. No matter the task, we worked together to get the job done. It was early to the field, often before the sun came up, and late back home, often after five o'clock. Lunch was very exciting, as it was set for noon, and Mama always came out to prepare the meal. It would get very hot before that time, but we were mentally prepared for the heat. Mama always made sure that we were dressed for the sun. We are very blessed not to have skin cancer because Mama was proactive by insisting that we wear long-sleeve shirts, long pants, and a hat to the field.

Notes:

21

Bringing Up the Cows and Feeding the Pigs

Bringing up the cows and feeding the pigs were some of our daily chores. The cows were always grazing in the back of the pasture and had to be brought into the stable in the evenings so they'd be close for the morning milking. I never learned how to milk a cow properly. I always had trouble manipulating the udders to get the milk to flow, so it would foam as it fell into the milk bucket. My sister, however, was an expert in the milking process.

The pigs had to be fed every morning before we left for school. Sometimes they did not cooperate. They often got out of the pen during the night, and we had to locate them before we could board the yellow school bus. Of course we always managed to get it all done in time to catch the bus. Sometimes it would be cold in the mornings, but we managed. We were determined to get as much done as we could in the morning before school so that the afternoon would be easier. There were not many free evenings after school. Mama, Daddy, or our grandfather always had something for us to work on when we returned from school.

Notes:

22

Butchering the Hogs and the Smokehouse

We always had one or two hogs to butcher, so that we would have meat for the winter and into the spring and the summer. Putting the hogs to rest was always a very special occasion in the winter months of November and December. In preparation for the big day, we cleaned the round black pot and placed it in a well-cleared area, where we'd heat up water over a wooden fire to keep the pot hot. The hot water was then used to clean the meat and the chitterlings. Then I did not know as much as I know now about the delicacy of chitterlings. Chitterlings are eaten boiled or fried and with hot sauce. In my earlier years, we only ate them fried. I learned the other ways to prepare them after moving to the Delta—the flatland area of the state.

We stored the meat in the smokehouse. My grandfather and daddy took care of the smokehouse and secured the meat for the winter months. They placed the meat—sausages, ham, and other types of meat—on a rack, where it would hang until it was cured and ready to be eaten by the family and shared with the community. It was always a joy to visit the smokehouse to get meat—better than going to the store. After leaving home, when I had to shop for groceries, it was very difficult to purchase meat from the market. The selection was not the same, and the taste not quite as good.

Notes:

19

***

Picking Peas and Cucumbers during the Summer

Peas and cucumbers were the fast cash crops in June and July. They grew fast and plentiful, which kept us busy. And the latter was exactly what Daddy wanted. We picked cucumbers for the market on Mondays, Wednesdays, and Fridays. Daddy would take them to what we called the cucumber vet for processing in the small town of Mt. Olive, Mississippi. We would often travel with him. In town, he would buy ice cream and sodas for us, and we would combine the two to make an ice cream soda float. If we did not ride with him, he would purchase the items and bring them with him so that we could make the floats at home. This was always such a treat. Mama also pickled and canned cucumbers in a jar for us to eat later during the winter months.

Pea picking was a delight. We picked them every day, some to sell and some for our own dinners and suppers. Shelling peas made your fingers turn purple and irritated them so much that they became tender. The pea-shelling activity didn't last long because we knew there was a new day to come and the process would start over again.

These chores helped us bond as a family because we worked together to get the job done. Selling peas and cucumbers helped my daddy and mama to have enough cash to purchase necessary items we did not produce on the farm.

Notes:

20

Dressed for the Sun

Growing up, we had to work the fields of our farm. Daddy always planted at least nine acres of cotton. He never said so, but we always figured that he planted one acre for each sibling to take care of. No matter the task, we worked together to get the job done. It was early to the field, often before the sun came up, and late back home, often after five o'clock. Lunch was very exciting, as it was set for noon, and Mama always came out to prepare the meal. It would get very hot before that time, but we were mentally prepared for the heat. Mama always made sure that we were dressed for the sun. We are very blessed not to have skin cancer because Mama was proactive by insisting that we wear long-sleeve shirts, long pants, and a hat to the field.

Notes:

23

Sunday Shoes

The black patent-leather shoes waited in the same place from one Sunday to the next, unless there was a revival going on during the week. They were referred to as the Sunday shoes because they were only worn on Sundays and because we polished them with bacon oil. It was a delight to have bacon on Sunday mornings because most of the time we had fried fish or fried chicken with gravy and rice. If there was no bacon, we used oil from the chicken to shine the patent-leather shoes. We also used the oil from the bacon and chicken to moisten our legs and other areas of the body that needed to look smooth and shiny.

Notes:

24

⟨⬦⟩

Riding the School Bus and Getting Frostbite

My siblings and I rode the bus to school each and every morning for more than thirty miles. During the winter months it was miserable. The bus did not have very much heat, if any. By the time we arrived at school, my feet would be very cold and frozen, and by evening they would be itching. My mother indicated that they were frostbitten. My feet would hurt and itch for several days because the cycle of freezing on the bus ride and thawing at school would continue throughout the winter.

Notes:

25

❖

My Grandfather and the Car

My daddy always had a truck because he was a farmer. We used the truck for everything, work and leisure travel, even for driving to church. It was convenient because we could spread out and sit in the back with the tailgate down and on the sides. Where you sat depended on your age. My daddy was very careful and cautious—he kept his eyes focused on the steering wheel, Mama, and those of us riding on the back of the truck. We had a fun time talking and visiting with each other as we traveled to church.

My maternal grandfather did not like the idea of the girls riding in the back of the truck. He indicated that we were getting dusty and that our hair was blowing out of place. He shared this information with my daddy, and it was not long after this conversation that my grandfather purchased a car for us. It was a green four-door Plymouth. It was supposed to protect our mother and his grandchildren from the elements. He was a thoughtful and caring grandfather, never to be forgotten.

Of course my dad was the driver, but he did not like it because it was crowded. We kept the car but mostly used the truck.

Notes:

26

❧

My First Grandchild

My first grandchild was born on a sunny but cool December 7, 1988, the day that Japan bombed Pearl Harbor in 1941. I was always told that my uncle J was preparing to come home from the war but had to delay his departure because of the surprise attack. My grandson entered this world in the early morning. He was and continues to be pleasant. He was told that his grandmother would be his caretaker and that he should call her Nana. That started a trend, and all of my grandchildren call me Nana. My first grandson is a very talented young man and a joy to be around. He now refers to himself as a jack-of-all-trades. He knows himself well. He hung around his grandmother and aunt until he was entering second grade. His mother always said that she was coming to get him, and he would prepare his favorite items for her arrival. If she did not show up, we would tell him that we would pack him in a box and send him to her. Of course we were joking. And then one day she arrived as promised. He was all packed and ready to go. We cried. His mother told us that he said, "I don't know why they are crying; they have said many times that they were going to pack me in a box and send me to you."

Notes:

27

Parching Corn

After harvesting season, the crib was full of corn, real corn, for many days. It was an adventure to go to the crib and look for small ears of corn to pop for popcorn. If not all of the kernels popped, it parched and was crunchy. We added salt to give it flavor. Daddy could not face the crunchy sound, so we just kept our distance from him while eating. It was a delicious night time treat. To this day popcorn is one of my favorite snacks.

Notes:

28

❦

Cooking Biscuits on the Open Fire

It is a kitchen chore to prepare the biscuits and place them in a pan to be baked in the oven. However, if you have done it many times, it gets easy. My mother did this many times using the oven in the kitchen, but when the butane gas was out, she would place the biscuits on the open fire or on the wood heater in Papa's room. Papa's room was a special place because it had a sofa. My mother would allow the biscuits to brown on one side and then turn them again and again until they were done. When they were brown on both sides and done, they were delicious, even better than the biscuits baked in the oven. The biscuits were always good with bacon, sausage, and syrup. Delicious.

Notes:

29

Roasting Potatoes over the Open Fire

Building a fire on a winter morning was always an eventful chore. The person in charge had to start a fire that had to burn all day and into the night. During the day, my grandfather would roast sweet potatoes for a snack, and during the evening, we would sit around the open fire and roast them for dinner. Those potatoes were the best.

Notes:

30

❖

Reading the Progressive Farmer

I read the *Progressive Farmer* early because I had learned to read by observing my dad and grandfather read the magazine. It arrived in the mail once per month and was a jewel for our house. Sometimes this was the only book we had because the public library in our small town was off limits to us, but we learned to read anyway. Today, children have so many books. Today, you don't have an excuse not to read. If I was able to learn to read by observing my grandfather and father read the *Progressive Farmer* and listening to my mother's advice, you can learn to read with the resources available in your immediate reach.

Notes:

31

<hr/>

Prince Albert Tobacco Can and the Spring Water

Growing up in the southern country with sprawling space to run and play was a gift given to us from our grandfather. We had a special place on his property, away from the main portion of the land, referred to as the low field. While working in the field in that area, in order to have water to drink, we had to take water with us. It was far from the main house, although there was a running spring with pure water that we would visit if we did not have water with us. It was an extra adventure to go with Daddy to the spring. We would sit by the spring and watch while he dipped a Prince Albert tobacco can in the spring to get the water. It was a treat to have pure springwater to drink. The springwater added to the tobacco can made an awesome and strong aroma. I can still smell the aroma from the Prince Albert tobacco to this day. We could not wait to return to the spring for more water to drink. The spring continues to exist to this day, but it has been a decade or more since I have visited it.

Lasting first experiences always linger with you forever.

Notes:

32

July Fourth Disappointment

We thought summertime, with plenty of farm and household chores to complete and no place to go, was a ritual. My daddy was a farmer and was always doing some farmwork. He was a slim man with curly hair and very few words, but he was an extraordinary listener. As he got older, his hair turned straight. He heard and read everything and could always hold an intelligent conversation. Daddy dedicated himself to keeping his children close to him, especially the girls. So we did not learn to drive as the boys did. Later we understood his reason for not teaching his daughters, and our mother to drive. It was to keep us at home to know our whereabouts most of the time. Mama always said she wanted to learn to drive, but she never did.

She shared with us on several occasions that once she wanted to attend Sunday morning and evening revival services at a church about thirty miles away. She had designed and sewn a multicolored flowered dress to wear that Sunday. Daddy knew of her plans, but he refused to drive her to church. This was his way to control the ladies close to him and know their whereabouts. Daddy died several years ago and left Mama with a car in the driveway without a driver. She refuses to sell it or give it away. We hope she will want to learn how to drive just for revenge.

However, it was a warm Fourth of July several years ago when we learned the worst of the worst lessons. My sisters and I had planned a trip to a nearby small town to visit with cousins and friends. We did not see these friends often but enjoyed socializing with them. We also had an aunt who lived on the circular street in the immediate area where we wanted to visit. Her children were grown and away from home, and we always looked forward to her company—and her cooking. She always kept baked sweet potatoes cut into wedges along with parched peanuts, which I enjoyed eating. They were always on the top of her stove.

As a seamstress, Mama had sewn each of us a pair of pink flowered shorts and a matching blouse to wear for the occasion. We had purchased the cloth to make the shorts and blouses with money we had earned picking cucumbers on the family farm. Daddy had plenty of work for us to do, which kept us from getting into trouble with each other.

We got dressed to go to town, but Daddy did not come in from the field until late. Daddy went to the field early that Fourth of July to plow and plowed from sunup to sundown in the bottom field. We would go to the top of the hill to check on his progress. We could not see him behind the billowing dust cloud around him, but we could tell that he was almost finished with the task. He was supposed to come to take us to town at 5:00 p.m., and we made sure we looked our best. However, Daddy did not come home until dark. We were beyond disappointed. We knew Mama was not going to let us go to town because it was too late. That was the worst day of my life. To this day, I do not make big plans, no matter the occasion.

From this life's lesson, I wrote the following poem:

> I remember the time my daddy plowed until nine.
> He kept us waiting and prevented the dating.
> He knew we were young and needed to be taught a song.
> The tune would be rhymes with patterns and symbols.
> A lifelong lesson was taught with pain and passion.
> We never planned without consent from the man—Daddy.

Notes:

33

A Daughter's Story

We always enjoyed visiting our grandparents, despite my mama's reluctance to drive. The gigantic lawn and the huge trees that provided shade in the summertime created a perfect place for us to run and play. When we were younger, my mom would allow us to take our tricycles and other toys for entertainment.

We stopped at McDonald's on the way to our grandparents' home. We had to have one or two of those mouth-watering burgers and fries. They were always good. After we had devoured the food, it was time to continue traveling to our grandparents' house. It always seemed to take forever to get there.

Grandmother appeared to always enjoy our visits at her house. She prepared the best meals, which often included fluffy biscuits and spicy homemade sausages that would melt in your mouth. Her homemade jelly would keep you coming back for more.

We didn't get the opportunity to spend much time with our grandparents, just weekends—and you know how short they are. We always left Sunday afternoon so we could get home before dark. Mama didn't like to drive at night. We were always sad because we knew it would be a long time before we returned.

Notes:

34

Parents' Story

Almost every summer, our three girls would journey to their grandparents' house for a week of fun with their cousins and friends. They looked forward to this week because it was a time for them to play outside until dark and get fresh popcorn popped on the stove by their second-oldest aunt. My mother and father always made sure that they followed our rules even in their house. My youngest daughter would always try to convince my parents to do something that she knew her father and I would object to. One time in particular my daughter wanted to go to the church to help her aunt Dot, but my mother was very strict and always made sure that if you were left with her, you stayed with her. Since my mother could not reach me to ask if I'd allow my daughter to go, she had to stay at home with my mother. My daughter often says that she cried and cried and received her first and last spanking from her grandmother Smith. As my youngest daughter got older, she tried to get out of going to church on Sundays while visiting and would leave her Sunday clothes at home. One thing was always understood: you went to church on Sundays, regardless of whether you wanted to or not. She had to go to church without her Sunday clothes. After all, she *was* dressed.

Notes:

35

Toe Stickers

Thongs—toe stickers, as we called them—as footwear are designed to be worn, not to be buried in white sand among rows of cotton in a cotton field. Several years ago, when thongs were new to me, I had a baby-blue pair that I purchased from an outside job—maybe chopping cotton for a nearby farmer. However, I did not keep the footwear for a long time.

As my sisters and I were chopping cotton on a hot, sunny day on a sandy hillside in view of the family home, I took a break from chopping cotton, pulled my toe stickers off, heaped a pile of white sand, and buried my pair of baby blues in it. I never found them again, not even after digging and digging deep into the sand. They were lost, really lost.

While attempting to find my toe stickers, my tender, small hands spread and smoothed the pile of white sand. My sisters helped ease my worries of not being able to find my shoes by telling me that I could get another pair. Their comforting spirit did not help me, though. I wanted that baby-blue pair. But they were lost—gone forever. It was a long time before I purchased another pair because I could not locate a pair that fit as well as my first, and none that carried the same meaning and importance. I did purchase a pair of pink thongs during spring break one March, but they did not have the same feel of comfort as my baby-blue ones.

Notes:

36

My Grandfather

My grandfather was a man who advised his family.
He read everything in sight.
He always had something to share about any topic.
He helped me to become a complete person.
My grandfather was a man who advised his family.

He was a caring and insightful man.
He read books, newspapers, magazines, and wrote letters to his friends.
He took notes as he read the Sunday school lessons.
He always had a story to tell.
My grandfather was a man who advised his family.

He was a teacher who taught all subjects.
He inferred situations that now I understand.
He was a man of positive character—good character.
My grandfather was a man who greatly inspired his family.
He was one who was admired by all.

Notes:

NOTES

NOTES

NOTES

NOTES